Faber Studio Collection

Selections from ChordTime Piano

Arranged by Nancy and Randall Faber

T0086920

This book belongs to: _____

Popular

Classics

Jazz & Blues

Rock 'n Roll

and more...

Production Coordinator: Jon Ophoff
Design and Illustration: Terpstra Design, San Francisco
Engraving: Dovetree Productions, Inc.

FABER
PIANO ADVENTURES®
3042 Creek Drive
Ann Arbor, Michigan 48108

A NOTE TO TEACHERS

The **Faber Studio Collections** offer a mix of styles with selections from the *PreTime®* to *BigTime®* Piano Supplementary Library. This sampling from the *Popular*, *Classics*, *Jazz & Blues*, *Rock 'n Roll*, and other favorite books presents an array of genres at each level. When a style resonates, the student can pick up just the right book for follow-up.

Not only is the **ChordTime® Faber Studio Collection** appealing to the student, it is especially formulated for the piano teacher! In keeping with the "ChordTime" concept, the songs are arranged to provide the student opportunity for chord recognition and chord practice, particularly of the I, IV, and V7 chords. The keys are limited to C, G, F, and G minor with warm-up exercises for each key. The teacher should feel free to skip around among the key sections.

The **ChordTime® Faber Studio Collection** is part of the *ChordTime® Piano* series. "ChordTime" designates Level 2B of the *PreTime®* to *BigTime® Piano Supplementary Library* arranged by Faber and Faber.

Following are the levels of the supplementary library, which lead from *PreTime®* to *BigTime®*.

PreTime® Piano	(Primer Level)
PlayTime® Piano	(Level 1)
ShowTime® Piano	(Level 2A)
ChordTime® Piano	(Level 2B)
FunTime® Piano	(Level 3A – 3B)
BigTime® Piano	(Level 4 and above)

Each level offers books in a variety of styles, making it possible for the teacher to offer stimulating material for every student. For a complimentary detailed listing, e-mail faber@pianoadventures.com or write us at the mailing address below.

Visit **www.PianoAdventures.com**.

ONLINE SUPPORT

Visit **www.PianoAdventures.com/studio** to find online support for this book!

ISBN 978-1-61677-643-5

TABLE OF CONTENTS

I, IV, V7 Chords in the Key of C

The Entertainer...4

What Makes You Beautiful...............................6

Do-Re-Mi (from *The Sound of Music*)................8

Crazy Little Thing Called Love.........................10

Yesterday...12

Pizzicato Polka...14

I, IV, V7 Chords in the Key of G

New River Train..16

Long, Long Ago..18

Tuxedo Junction...20

I, IV, V7 Chords in the Key of F

Amazing Grace...22

Watermelon Man..24

Polovetzian Dance No. 17...............................26

I, IV, V7 Chords in the Key of G Minor

Havah Nageela...28

Music Dictionary...32

Key of C

Practice these warm-ups before playing the songs in the key of C.

Warm-up 1

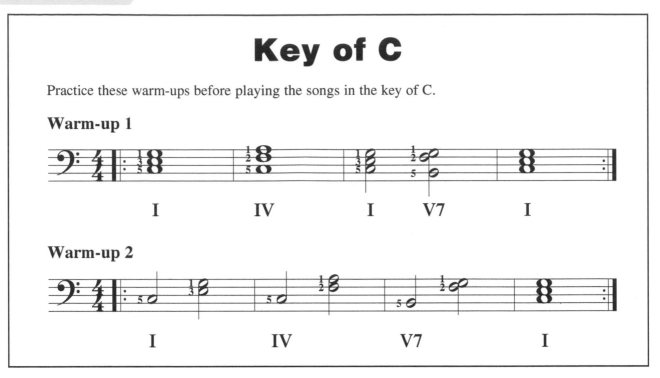

Warm-up 2

The Entertainer

SCOTT JOPLIN

FF30

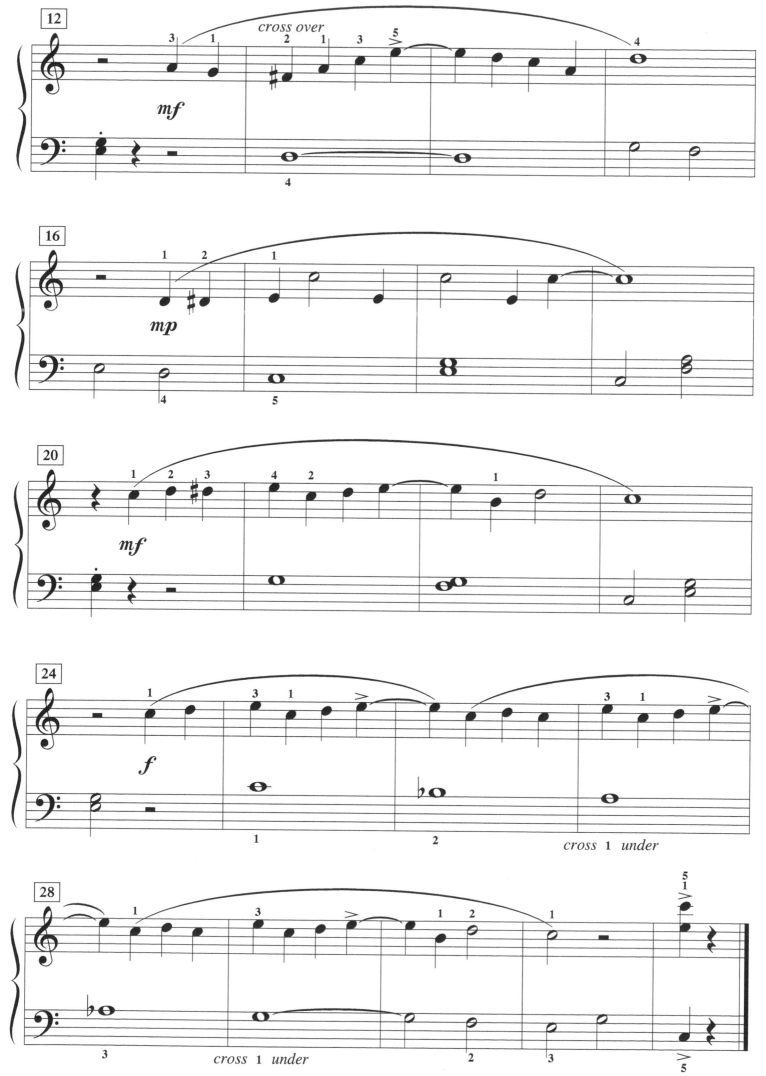

What Makes You Beautiful

Words and Music by SAVAN KOTECHA,
RAMI YACOUB and CARL FALK

FF301

from *The Sound of Music*

Do-Re-Mi

Lyrics by OSCAR HAMMERSTEIN II
Music by RICHARD RODGERS

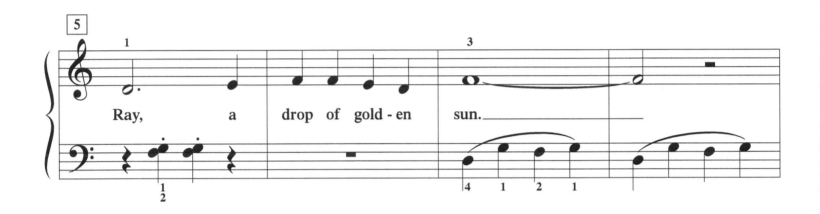

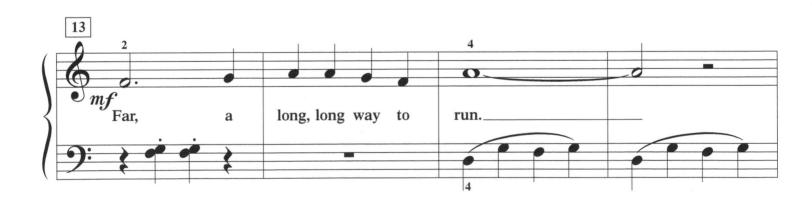

FF30

Crazy Little Thing Called Love

Words and Music by
FREDDIE MERCURY

FF301

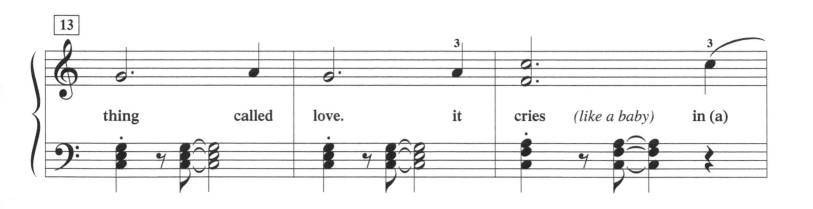

thing called love. it cries *(like a baby)* in (a)

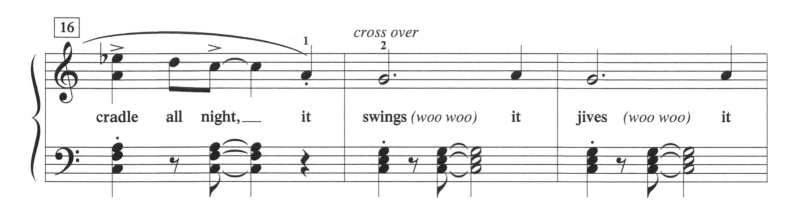

cross over

cradle all night,___ it swings *(woo woo)* it jives *(woo woo)* it

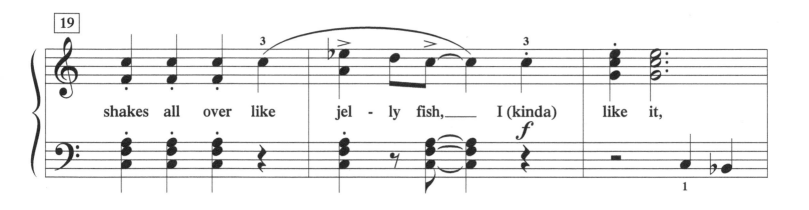

shakes all over like jel - ly fish,___ I (kinda) like it,

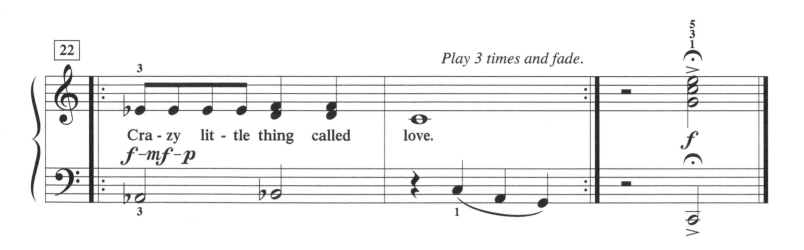

Play 3 times and fade.

Cra - zy lit - tle thing called love.

f—mf—p

Yesterday

Words and Music by
JOHN LENNON and PAUL McCARTNEY

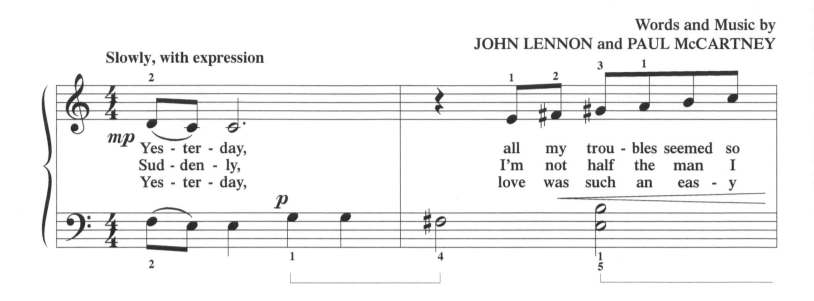

FF301

Why   she   had   to   go   I   don't

know,   she would-n't   say.   I   said

D.C. al Coda

some - thing wrong, now I   long   for yes - ter - day.

Coda

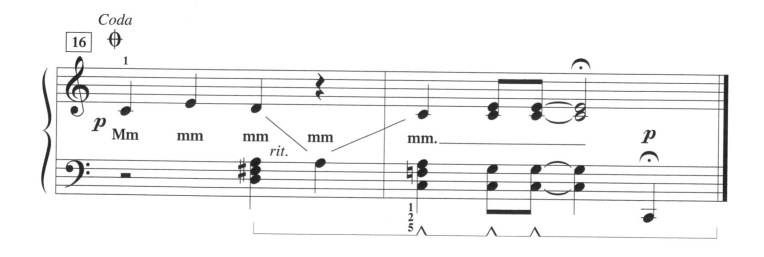

Mm   mm   mm   mm   mm.

rit.

Pizzicato Polka

JOHANN STRAUSS, JR.
(1825-1899)
and JOSEF STRAUSS
(1827-1870)

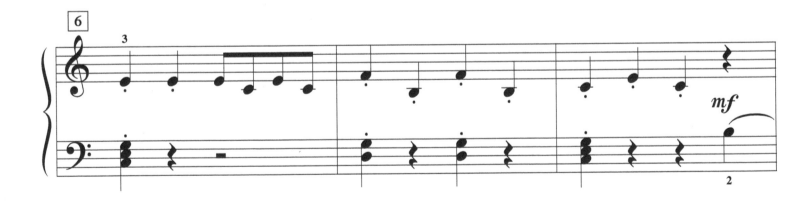

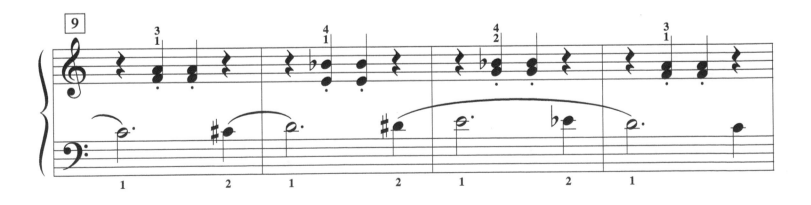

FF301

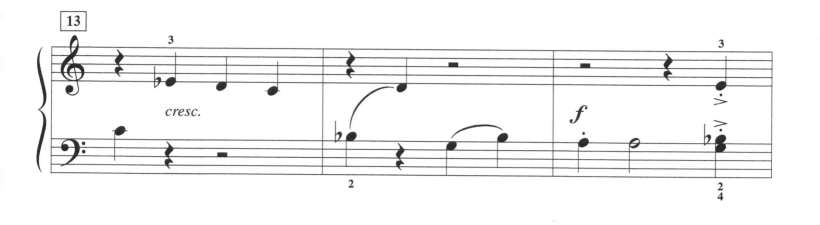

Key of G

Practice these warm-ups before playing the songs in the key of G.

Warm-up 1

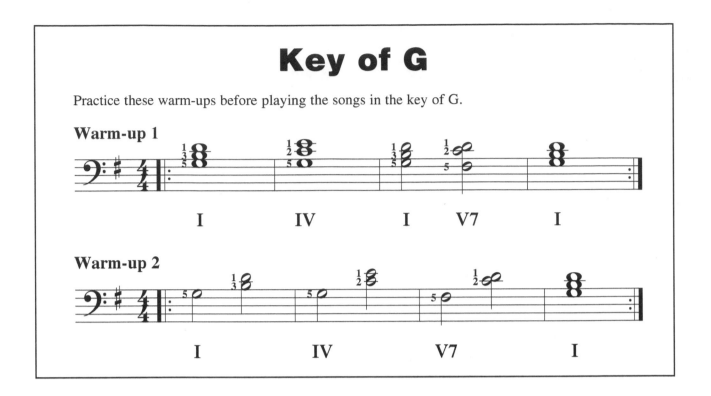

I   IV   I   V7   I

Warm-up 2

I   IV   V7   I

New River Train

Lively

GOSPEL

FF30

Long, Long Ago

THOMAS H. BAYLY

Smoothly

mp Tell me the tales that to me were so dear,

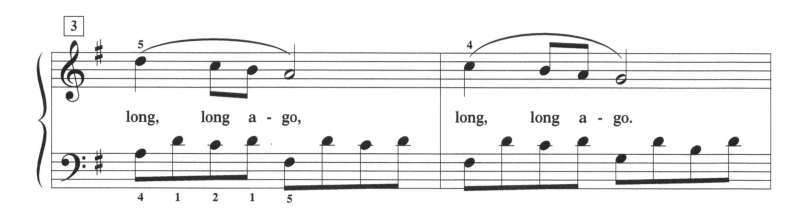

long, long a - go, long, long a - go.

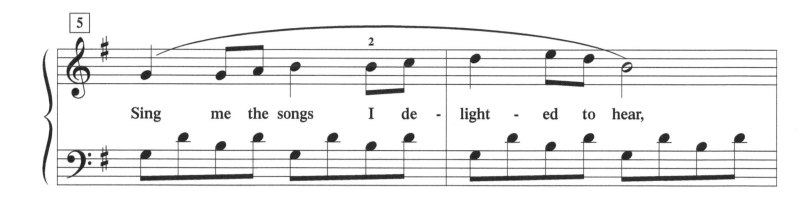

Sing me the songs I de - light - ed to hear,

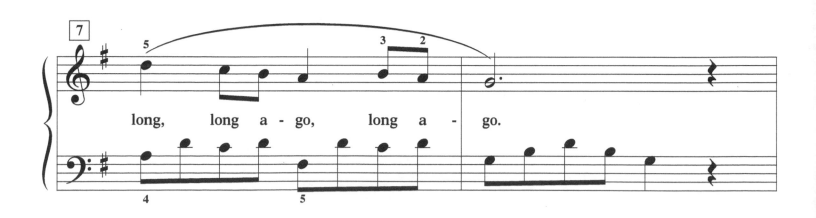

long, long a - go, long a - go.

FF301

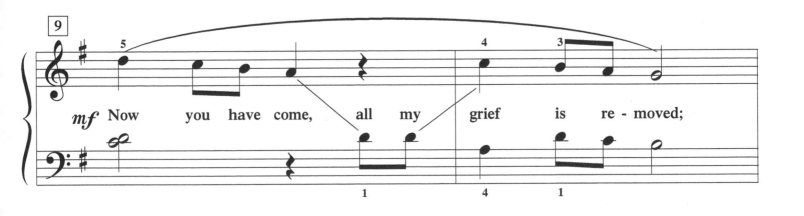

Now you have come, all my grief is re - moved;

Let me for - get that so long you have roved.

Let me be - lieve that you love as you loved,

long, long a - go, long a - go. *rit.*

Tuxedo Junction

Words by
BUDDY FEYNE

Music by ERSKINE HAWKINS,
WILLIAM JOHNSON, and JULIAN DASH

FF301

Key of F

Practice these warm-ups before playing the songs in the key of F.

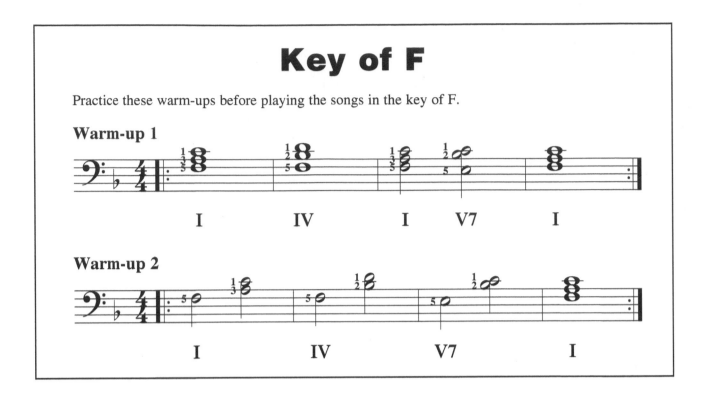

Amazing Grace

Text – JOHN NEWTON
Tune – EARLY AMERICAN

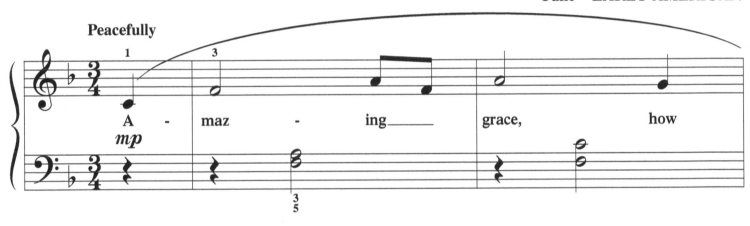

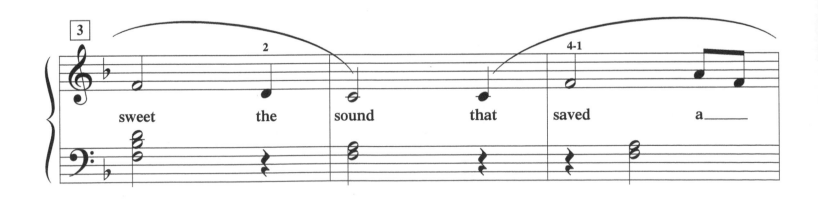

FF30

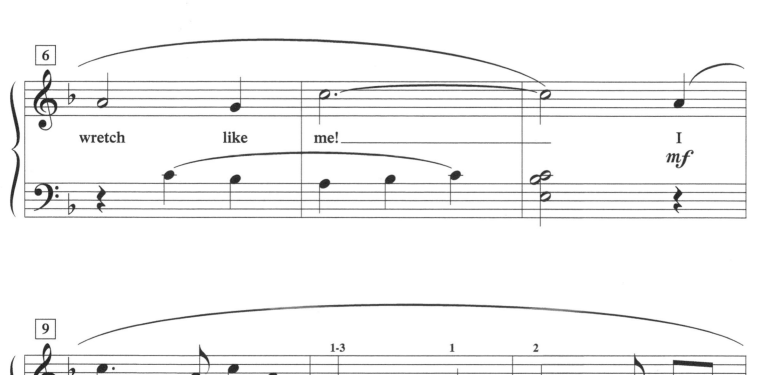

wretch like me! I

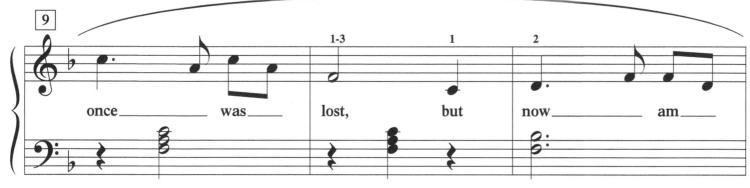

once was lost, but now am

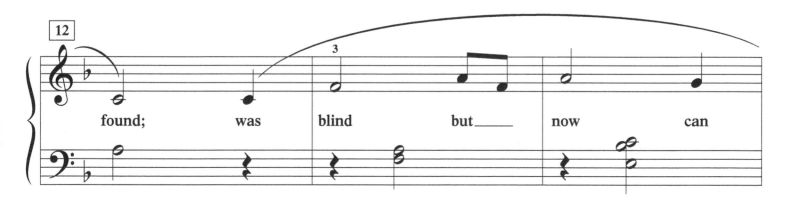

found; was blind but now can

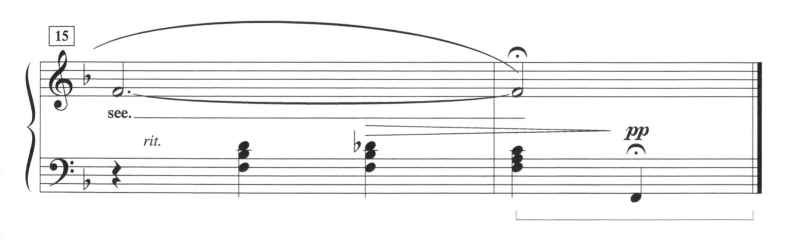

see.

Watermelon Man

Laid back

By HERBIE HANCOCK

FF301

Polovetzian Dance No. 17

(from the opera *Prince Igor*)

ALEXANDER BORODIN
(1833-1887)

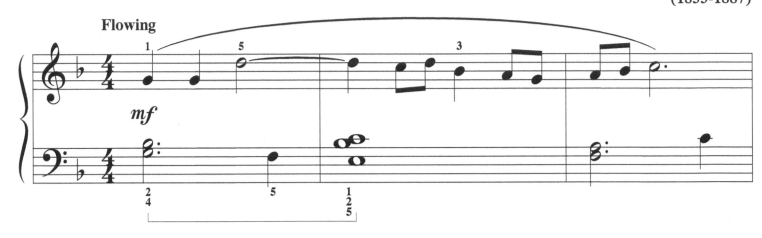

FF30

Key of G Minor

Practice these warm-ups before playing this song in the key of G minor.

Warm-up 1

i iv i V⁷ i

Warm-up 2

i iv V⁷ i

(Whole line, 2 times) הָבָה נָגִילָה (3 times) וְנִשְׂמְחָה
(Whole line, 2 times) הָבָה נְרַנְּנָה (3 times) וְנִשְׂמְחָה
עוּרוּ עוּרוּ אַחִים
(4 times) עוּרוּ אַחִים בְּלֵב שָׂמֵחַ
עוּרוּ אַחִים עוּרוּ אַחִים, בְּלֵב שָׂמֵחַ

Teacher Note: Courtesy accidentals are included for students who
may be unfamiliar with this key signature.

Havah Nageela
(Hora*)
הָבָה נָגִילָה

TRADITIONAL

Lively

Ha - vah   na - gee - lah,   ha - vah   na - gee - lah

mf

(pedal optional)

cross over

ha - vah   na - gee - lah   v' - nis - m' - ḥah.

* The *hora* is a lively Israeli circle dance brought from Eastern Europe by early Jewish settlers in Palestine.

FF301

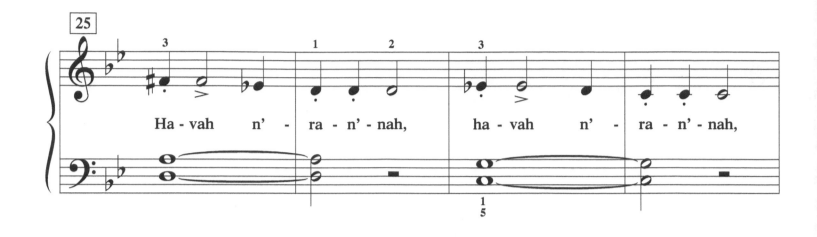

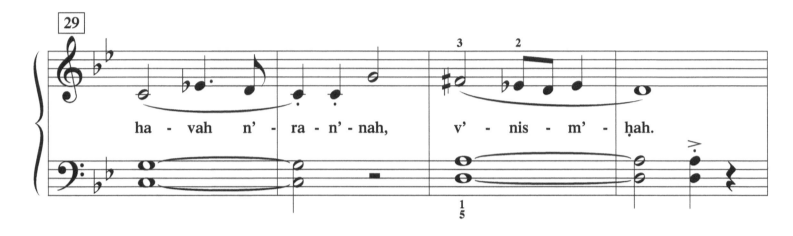

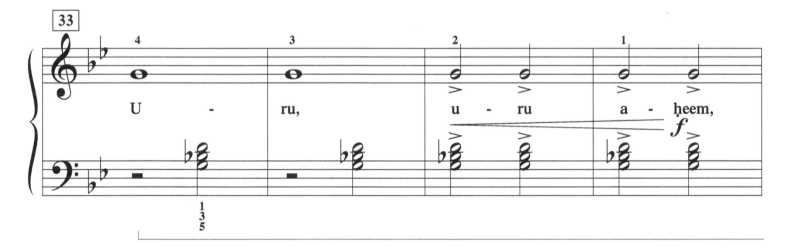

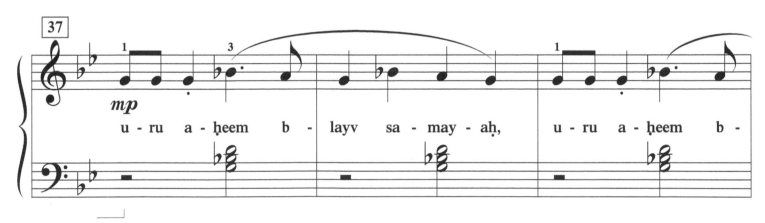

layv sa - may - ah u - ru a - heem b - layv sa - may - ah

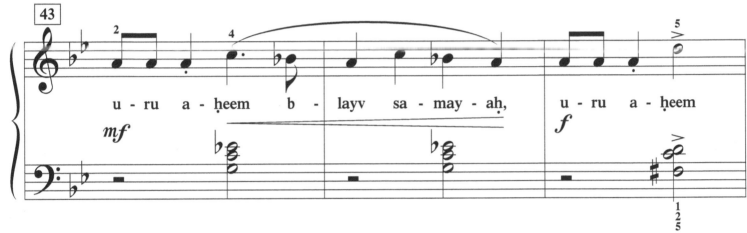

u - ru a - heem b - layv sa - may - ah, u - ru a - heem

mf *f*

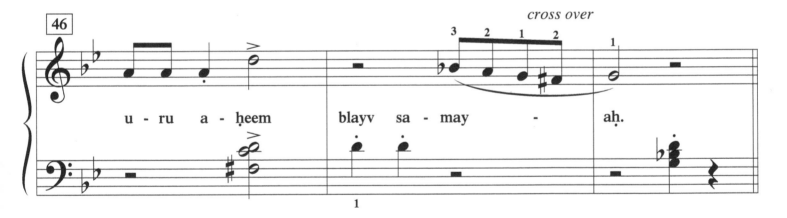

u - ru a - heem blayv sa - may - ah.

cross over

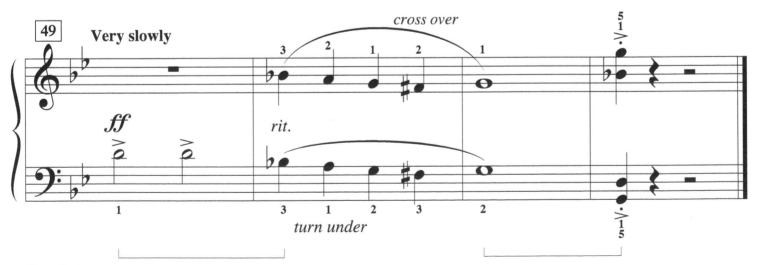

Very slowly *cross over*

ff *rit.*

turn under

Translation:
Come, let us rejoice and be happy.
Rouse yourselves up, brothers (and sisters), with a happy heart.

MUSIC DICTIONARY

p	mp	mf	f
piano	*mezzo piano*	*mezzo forte*	*forte*
soft	medium soft	medium loud	loud

crescendo (cresc.)
Play gradually louder.

diminuendo (dim.) or *decrescendo (decresc.)*
Play gradually softer.

SIGN	TERM	DEFINITION
>	**accent**	Play this note louder.
⊕	*Coda*	Ending section.
¢	*Cut Time*	₂/₂ time. 2 half note beats per measure. A ♩ instead of a ♩ receives the beat.
D.C. al Coda	*Da Capo al Coda*	Return to the beginning and play to ⊕, then jump to the *Coda* (ending).
D.S.	*Dal Segno*	"From the sign." Return to the 𝄋 sign and play to the end.
𝄋	*segno*	See above.
𝄐	*fermata*	Hold this note longer than usual.
1. ⌐ 2. ⌐	**1st and 2nd endings**	Play the 1st ending and take the repeat. Then play the 2nd ending, skipping over the 1st ending.
♪	**grace note**	An ornamental note that is played quickly into the note that follows.
🎼♯ or 🎼♭	**key signature**	The key signature indicates the sharps or flats to be played for the key of the piece (major or minor). It is written at the beginning of each line of music.
8*va* ⌐	*ottava*	Play one octave higher than written. When 8*va* ⌐ is below the staff, play one octave lower.
⌞___⌟	**pedal mark**	Depress the damper (right-foot pedal) after the note or chord.
___∧___	**pedal change**	Lift the damper pedal as the note is played. Depress the pedal immediately after.
I, IV, V⁷	**primary chords**	These are the names for the three most common chords in any key: **I** is the Roman numeral for 1 (**i** for minor). **IV** is the Roman numeral for 4 (**iv** for minor). **V** is the Roman numeral for 5.
15*ma* ⌐	*quindicesima*	Play two octaves higher than written.
𝄆 ⋮ ⋮ 𝄇	**repeat signs**	Play the section within the repeat signs again.
rit.	*ritardando (ritard.)*	Gradually slow down.
⌢	**slur**	Connect the notes within a slur.
♪̇	*staccato*	Play *staccato* notes detached, disconnected.
	swing rhythm	Eighth notes played in a long-short pattern. (♫ = ♩³♪)

FF301